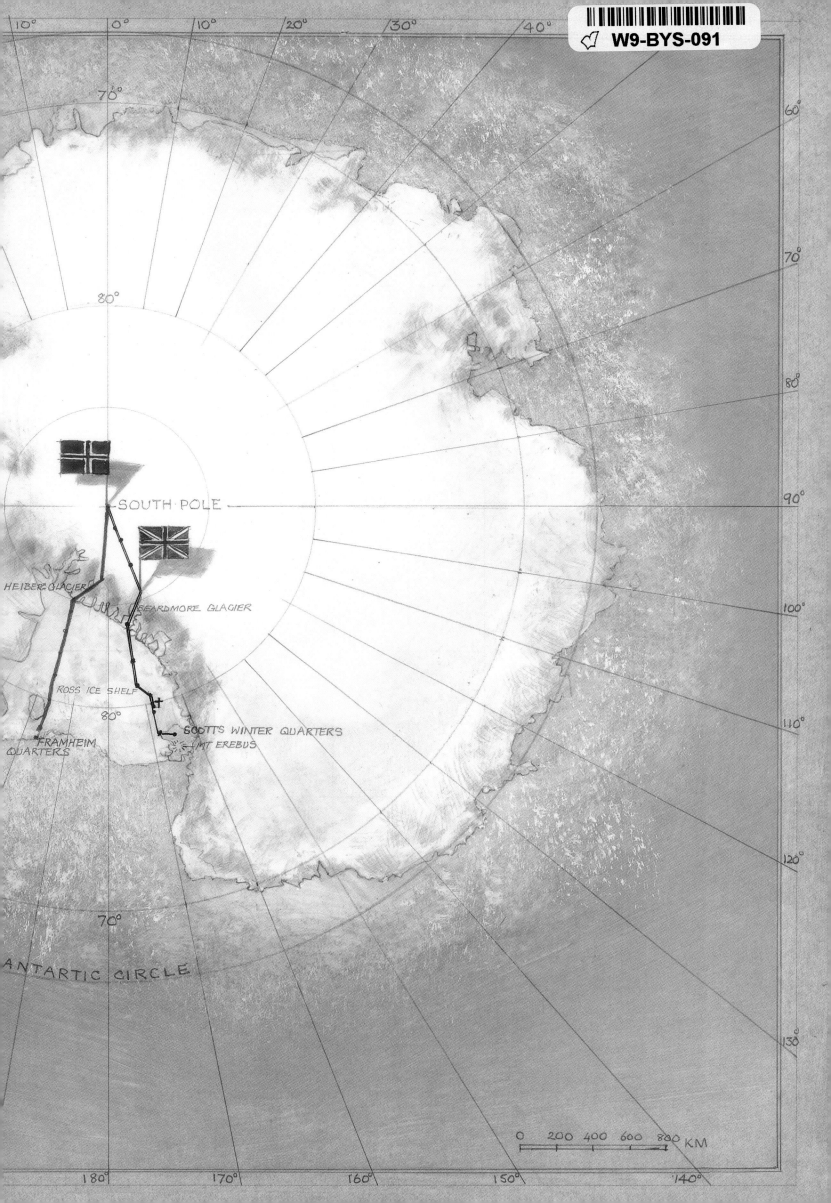

70°
0°
10°
20°
30°
40°
60°
70°
80°
90°
100°
110°
120°
130°
140°

70°
80°

SOUTH POLE

HEIBERG GLACIER

BEARDMORE GLACIER

ROSS ICE SHELF

80°

SCOTT'S WINTER QUARTERS

FRAMHEIM QUARTERS

MT EREBUS

70°

ANTARTIC CIRCLE

180°
170°
160°
150°
140°

0  200  400  600  800 KM

# ROBERT SCOTT

Mason Crest Publishers, Inc.
370 Reed Road
Broomall, Pennsylvania 19008
866-MCP-BOOK (toll free)

Illustrations copyright © 1998 Robert Ingpen
Published in association with
Grimm Press Ltd., Taiwan

1 3 5 7 9 8 6 4 2

Library of Congress Cataloging-in-Publication Data:

on file at the Library of Congress.

ISBN 1-59084-146-8
ISBN 1-59084-133-6 (series)

*Great Names*

# ROBERT SCOTT

**Mason Crest Publishers**
Philadelphia

There is a place on this earth that no matter which way you look everywhere is north. That place is called the South Pole.

The South Pole lies on a continent locked in the "ice age." As large as Europe and America put together, less that 1 percent of it has ever been visited by human beings.

Many explorers have been drawn to this mysterious, icy continent. One of the most dramatic stories it has produced is that of the race between Robert Scott and Roald Amundsen. Both men wanted to be the first to reach the South Pole. Both were courageous, determined, skilled, and hardy. Their successes and failures combine to weave an intensely moving and heroic tale.

Scott was a commander in the Royal Navy. He led two expeditions to the South Pole. On the first, Captain Ernest Shackleton and Dr. Edward Wilson joined him. The three set off from their base with 19 dogs on November 2, 1902. They walked for seven weeks through endless plains and towering mountains of ice. After traveling 373 miles (600 km), they were finally forced to turn back. Their dogs had died one after the other, and if it had not been for a strong tail wind, they too would have died on the return journey.

This first journey convinced Scott that dogs were of no use on the ice, when in fact, he had not cared for his dogs properly. He also felt that the use of dogs was cruel and not fitting with Royal Navy tradition. As a result, he decided he would use ponies and men to pull the sledges in the future journeys. This was a fatal error.

His second journey to the South Pole began in London on June 1, 1910. The journey's aims were twofold: to undertake further scientific research and

to plant the English flag at the Pole. A year earlier the North Pole had been won by an American, Robert Peary, causing Scott to write, "What matters now is that the South Pole should be attained by an Englishman."

Five days later, on June 6th, in Norway, a long-faced man with a well-bred mustache and quick, intelligent eyes boarded his ship, the *Fram*. This was Scott's rival, the experienced polar explorer Amundsen.

At age 15, Amundsen had decided he wanted to become an explorer and conquer the North Pole. However, his mother insisted he study medicine, which he did. But two years into the course, his mother died. He immediately abandoned his studies and set off in search of his dreams.

As the *Fram* drew away from the wharf, Amundsen's team stood on the deck and cheered, "North Pole, here we come!" In the half-light of morning, his men could not have seen the smile that flickered across Amundsen's face as he echoed, "Yes, here we come."

The *Fram* sailed first to a small island off the coast of South Norway, where they took on 100 or so dogs. The men were puzzled. "If we're going to the North Pole, why aren't we picking up dogs in Alaska?" "Who knows? Ask Amundsen," was the only reply.

Then, on September 9th, Amundsen called everyone together.

"We worked for two years in order to be the first to reach the North Pole, but Peary has beaten us and the American flag flies over it. Now the English plan to plant their flag at the South Pole. Are we going to sit back and let them?

We can beat them, so let's do it. We'll put the Norwegian flag at the South Pole. What do you say?" Stunned silence greeted the end of his speech, but after a moment's hesitation, the man happily agreed to head for the South Pole.

Scott's ship the *Terra Nova* was en route to Antarctica, when Scott received a telegram. It said, "Beg leave inform you proceeding Antarctic." Waving it angrily, Scott burst out, "This is ridiculous! We're not going to the Antarctic to take part in a race. We're going to conduct a scientific exploration."

"If he wants a race, that's his problem.  He's only got eight men and a pack of dogs. He doesn't stand a chance against us and our 17 ponies, 30 dogs, and three motor sleds," put in the others.

"He doesn't realize dogs are useless, either, and that will cost him dearly," added Scott. "But, with or without him, we will complete our mission with honor: the English way."

In January 1911, the *Terra Nova* arrived in the Antarctic. Scott's team set up base camp at McMurdo Sound, where they would await the following summer.

Amundsen had the same plan. The *Fram* arrived in the Antarctic in January, and Amundsen's team set up base camp in Whales Bay. They called their camp Framheim.

Framheim was 789 miles (1270 km) from the South Pole, 86 miles (140 km) closer than Scott's base. Although this route was shorter, it had never been tried before and so it presented many unknown dangers. Scott's route, on the other hand, had been traveled by Shackleton in 1908 and had taken him within 109 miles (175 km) of the South Pole.

The trip to the pole was a long one and would require more supplies than they could transport with them. So, in the six weeks of light left before the arrival of winter, Amundsen and his men hurried to establish supply depots along the route they would take south.

They set out with three sledges pulled by 18 dogs. The dogs made fast progress on the flat, snow-covered ground and in four days they arrived at latitude 81° South where they established a second supply depot. Again they returned and again they set out, for latitude 82° South and a third depot. Finally back at their base again, they began the long seven-week wait for the challenge ahead.

During this time, Scott's team also built supply depots. They used 13 men, 8 ponies, and 26 dogs, but the ponies' hooves sank deeply into the snow.

The ponies were so slow that they had to set off every day a good two hours before the dogs. And at night, while the dogs rested warmly in holes they dug in the snow, the ponies stood shivering in the biting –4° F (–20° C) winds.

One of the team members, Oates, said to Scott, "Captain, several of the ponies are ill and unable to go on. It would be kinder to kill them and use the meat to feed the dogs or us." But Scott was outraged at the suggestion. "The ponies are our friends. I am not going to kill them!" Three days later, two of the ponies were dead.

It took Scott and his men 24 days to reach 80° South. They left a large supply of food there, planted a black flag at the site, and headed back for Cape Evans. Winter at the pole is not only cold, it is also dark. There is no daylight, only night, and nothing to distinguish breakfast from dinner.

Although waiting, Amundsen's team was not idle. They worked hard on improving their ski equipment and taking care of the dogs. They watched slide shows to keep them from becoming depressed in the perpetual blackness.

Over at Scott's base, no one maintained the mechanical sledges and no one did any skiing. They watched movies, read books, and even produced a small newspaper, *The South Pole Times,* to wile away the dark hours. On August 23rd, the first rays of sunlight marked the end of winter, but it was still –58° F (–50° C), far too cold for anyone to travel.

The explorers all wanted to be the first to conquer the South Pole, but they had another important task as well—scientific research. Scott's team, in particular, made many significant contributions to meteorology, geology, cartography, and the study of glaciers.

By September 8th the temperature had risen to –35° F (–37° C), and Amundsen decided to make a start. The team, 8 men, 7 sledges, and 86 dogs, began their journey south across the snow.

Things went smoothly at first, and they covered 17.5 (28 km) miles a day. But on the third day the temperature dropped suddenly to –63° F (–53° C), and a dense white fog arrived. They could barely see a foot in front of them, but still they managed to travel at a pace of 17.5 miles a day.

The most experienced member of the team, Johansen complained angrily, "I told you it was too early to start. Do you want us to die out here? We've got to go back and wait until it is warmer." Amundsen was angry, with Johansen and with himself, for he knew that Johansen was right.

"All right," he agreed. "We'll go to the depot at 80° South, leave our supplies there, and then return to base." The return journey was much faster. Riding the now empty sledge, they literally raced back. Amundsen and two of his team led the way, covering the 45.5 miles (75 km) in just nine hours.

That afternoon, they were back at Framheim. Two hours later, the next group arrived. But Johansen's group had been left far behind. Their dogs were tired, cold, and wet, and they had no food. Staggering alone through the −58° F (−50° C) night, they finally reached the base around midnight.

The next morning Johansen criticized Amundsen in front of everyone, "You're not fit to be in charge! You left us behind without a thought for our safety. I'd be a better leader than you."

That evening Amundsen wrote Johansen a letter. It said, "You're not coming with me to the South Pole. I'll give you some dogs and you can go to King Edward VII Land. You can be the first person to go there."

On October 20th, Amundsen set off again. This time the party consisted of five men, four sledges, and 48 dogs. On November 12th they were ready to begin the 1.8 mile (3 km) climb to the polar plateau, up the dangerous Axel Heilberg Glacier. In four days, they traveled 50 miles (81 km) to the top.

Here Amundsen decided to kill all the dogs except for the 18 he needed to pull the three sledges. Their meat would be used to feed the other dogs and the men. It was a terrible decision to have to make, but probably the only choice they had.

Then, suddenly, the weather turned bad. Days of wind and snow were followed by thick fog. On one glacier pitted with hundreds of crevices, they nearly lost their way. But the glacier was beautiful. Icy blue, green, and white, it was a truly magnificent place. On this frightening yet beautiful glacier, Amundsen and his team spent four days but traveled only 5.5 miles (9 km).

The sun came out again, and on December 14th, Amundsen and his team arrived at 90° South. They planted the Norwegian flag into the ground and became the first people in history to stand at the South Pole.

They remained at the pole for two days. When they left, they left behind a tent, some spare supplies, a letter to the King of Norway, and a message for Scott. The 789-mile (1270-km) journey back to Framheim took them 99 days.

Scott didn't set off until November 3rd, two weeks after Amundsen. The
motor sledges soon broke down and had to be abandoned. The ponies' hooves
sank deeply into the snow, slowing them down to no more than 5.5 miles
(13 km) a day.

When they arrived at the Beardmore Glacier, Scott was forced to shoot his five surviving ponies. At this point, he sent four men and the dogs back to base, and divided the others into three groups of four. Each group was to pull one sledge behind them up the glacier. The men began their ascent—and while they were climbing, Amundsen reached the South Pole.

Once at the top, Scott sent a second group back to base and sometime further on, a third. However, he decided to keep Bowers with them. This meant that there were now five men in the final team but supplies for only four.

A Norwegian flag awaited Scott at the pole.

On January 17 1912, Scott found the flag, the tent, the food, and the letters Amundsen had left. The message to Scott read:

*Dear Captain Scott,*
*As you probably are the first to reach this area after us, I will ask you kindly to forward this letter to King Haakon VII. If you can use any of the supplies left in the tent, please do not hesitate to do so. I wish you a safe return.*
*Yours truly,*

*Roald Amundsen*

Scott wrote in his diary: "The South Pole. We've made it. . . . It is a terrible day. We are tired. Our hands and feet are frozen. Outside it is –30° F (–34° C). Great God, what an awful place! To have endured so much and not to be the first, is a terrible disappointment."

The five tired men stood downcast in the coldest, emptiest place on earth.

Scott didn't hurry back to his base; in fact, he even spent time collecting rock samples along the way. The men were always hungry. There were too few supply depots and a single black flag was hard to find in the thick snow.

Evans moved more and more slowly and fell further and further behind. They put him on one of the sledges, but he was exhausted. He died after a fall on the ice.

Oates was suffering too. His feet were numb, swollen, and black.

March 17th was Oates' birthday. Outside the tent, the wind was howling and the temperature was a freezing −40° F (−40° C). Oates struggled to his feet and handed a letter he had written to his mother to Wilson. He said, "I'm just going outside and may be some time."

Oates stumbled out into the snow and wind and was never seen again. Scott wrote: "Oates died like a good Englishman. It is the way we would all wish to die—we know that the end is not far."

Scott, Wilson, and Bowers were trapped by a snowstorm no more than 10.5 miles (17 km) from their next supply depot.

They could go no further. Scott wrote 11 dignified and moving letters to family and friends and one to the British people in which he proudly said: "We have shown that Englishmen can endure hardships, help one another, and meet death with as great a fortitude as ever in the past."

From his letters, we know that their food and fuel was exhausted and their feet and hands were frozen. Yet he wrote, "If you were here with us in this tent, you would hear us singing. . . . Had we lived, I should have had a tale to tell of hardihood, endurance, and courage of my companions.

"I do not regret this journey. We took risks and we knew we took them; things have come out against us, and therefore we have no cause for complaint, but bow to the will of Providence, determined still to do our best to the last."

On March 29, 1912, Scott wrote in his diary for the last time: "Please remember us. . . . We did our best."

Amundsen and his team returned safely. The news of their success spread quickly and they were hailed as heroes. No one yet knew that Scott, Wilson, and Bowers were dead on the polar ice.

Winter's blackness descended again on the South Pole and snowflakes settled on the frozen bodies of three men in a battered tent.

The skill and determination of those who succeed fills the world with admiration; and the tragic courage of those who fail moves us deeply.

# BIOGRAPHIES

Author John Riddle is a freelance writer from Bear, Delaware. His byline has appeared in the *Washington Post,* the *New York Times, Boston Magazine,* and dozens of other publications. He is the author of *Consulting Business* and *Streetwise Guide to Business Management.* He is a frequent speaker at writing conferences around the country.

Illustrator Robert Ingpen was born in 1936 in Geelong, Australia. Ingpen's earliest work was the sketch of a shell he did when he was young. His first job, at the age of 22, was to draw illustrations and design publicity pamphlets for CSIRO, a scientific research institution. All of his illustrations were related to various scientific research reports. The work honed his perception and established his realistic style of painting. Interestingly, Ingpen's illustrations sometimes inspired scientists to explore and study the subject at hand from new perspectives. This is where the charm of Ingpen lies.